OUR HOLIDAY SYMBOLS

Easter Bunnies

by Patrick Merrick

Published by The Child's World®
1980 Lookout Drive
Mankato, MN 56003-1705
800-599-READ
www.childsworld.com

ACKNOWLEDGMENTS
The Child's World®: Mary Berendes, Publishing Director

The Design Lab: Kathleen Petelinsek, Design

Editorial Directions, Inc.: E. Russell Primm, Editorial Director; Joshua Gregory, Editorial Assistant;
Jennifer Zeiger, Fact Checker; Lucia Raatma, Copyeditor and Proofreader

PHOTO CREDITS
Cover and page 1, ©iStockphoto.com; page 5, ©Monika Gniot, used under license from Shutterstock, Inc.;
page 7, ©iStockphoto.com/melissaperryphotography; page 9, ©libby j hansen, used under license from
Shutterstock, Inc.; page 11, ©Hway Kiong Lim, used under license from Shutterstock, Inc.; page 13, ©Ele-
na Blokhina, used under license from Shutterstock, Inc.; page 15, ©iStockphoto.com/pershinghks; page 17,
©iStockphoto.com/hartcreations; page 19, ©Vera Tomankova, used under license from Shutterstock, Inc.;
page 21, ©iStockphoto.com/ArtisticCaptures

LIBRARY OF CONGRESS CATALOGING-IN-PUBLICATION DATA
Merrick, Patrick.
  Easter bunnies / by Patrick Merrick.
    p. cm. — (Our holiday symbols)
  Includes bibliographical references and index.
  ISBN 978-1-60253-333-2 (library bound : alk. paper)
  1. Easter Bunny—Juvenile literature. 2. Easter eggs—Juvenile literature. I. Title. II. Series.
  GT4935.4.M37 2010
  394.2667—dc22   2009035308

Printed in the United States of America
Mankato, Minnesota
November 2009
F11460

Table of Contents

Spring Is in the Air!

People look forward to the first signs of spring. The weather starts to get warmer. Robins and bluebirds start appearing. Baseball season begins. People go on picnics. Many people wait for one special **holiday** to let them know spring has started. That day is Easter!

Spring is a time of new life. Flowers begin to bloom, and young animals are born.

What Is Easter?

Easter is a **religious** holiday for **Christians**. They celebrate by going to church.

Easter is on a different date every year. The date depends on when there is a full moon. The date is always on a Sunday. It is also always between March 22 and April 25.

People who go to church on Easter Sunday often dress in their best clothes. Some people even buy new outfits just for the holiday.

7

Do Many People Celebrate Easter?

Easter is a major holiday in many places around the world. Christians go to church. Many people celebrate the day with treats such as chocolate candy and Easter eggs. Who brings these brightly colored eggs and tasty candies? It's the Easter Bunny!

The Easter Bunny is a well-known **symbol** of Easter. Everyone loves the treats he brings!

What Is the Easter Bunny?

People used to believe that a goddess called Eastre was in charge of bringing spring. Spring would not come if Eastre was unhappy. Winter would last forever!

People had parties for Eastre to make sure she was happy. Eastre's favorite animal was the **hare**. Hares are a lot like Easter bunnies!

Hares look a lot like rabbits. They are actually a different kind of animal, though.

We no longer believe in Eastre. We know that spring always comes after winter. We still have the Easter Bunny, though!

Bunnies are a symbol of new life. Baby animals are born in spring. Flowers begin to grow. The Easter Bunny brings more than just spring. He also brings eggs!

Baby bunnies look different from full-grown rabbits. They are smaller, and their fur is fuzzier.

What Kinds of Eggs Does the Easter Bunny Bring?

The Easter Bunny brings eggs that are colored with **dye**. Sometimes they are decorated, too. We use fancy Easter baskets to hold the eggs that the Easter Bunny brings. Sometimes the Easter Bunny also brings chocolate candy and small presents. These are for the children who have been very good during the winter!

Coloring Easter eggs is a fun holiday activity for many people. Eggs can be painted with all kinds of different colors and designs.

15

What Does the Easter Bunny Do?

The Easter Bunny brings treats to children all over the world. Different places have different Easter **traditions**. In some places, the Easter Bunny puts eggs in the children's baskets. In other places, he hides the eggs. Then the children have to go on an Easter-egg hunt!

Easter-egg hunts can be a lot of fun. You never know what kinds of hiding places the Easter Bunny will come up with!

Should You Buy Easter Bunnies?

Many places sell baby rabbits during the Easter season. People want to buy them because they are so cute. This is not a good idea. Taking care of a rabbit is a lot of work! You should buy one only if you are ready to care for it.

It is easy to see why someone would want a cute baby rabbit for a pet. It is not easy to be a rabbit owner, though.

Is There Really an Easter Bunny?

Is the Easter Bunny real? Has anyone ever seen him? Some people say he is real. Other people say he is not. Everyone agrees on one thing, though. The Easter Bunny comes to spread fun and happiness every spring!

The Easter Bunny brings treats and springtime cheer. Maybe that is why everyone likes him so much!

Glossary

Christians (KRIS-chunz) Christians have a set of beliefs about God that are based on the teachings of Jesus. Christians celebrate Easter every year.

dye (DIE) A dye is a liquid that is used to color things. Clothes and Easter eggs are colored with dye.

hare (HAYR) A hare is an animal that looks and acts a lot like a rabbit.

holiday (HOL-uh-day) A holiday is a special day that people celebrate every year. Easter is a holiday.

religious (ruh-LIH-jus) When something is religious, it has to do with a religion, such as Christianity or Judaism.

symbol (SIM-bull) A symbol is an object that stands for something else. Bunnies are a symbol of the warmth and new life of spring.

traditions (tra-DIH-shunz) A tradition is a way of doing things. Traditions are passed down from year to year.

Books and Web Sites

BOOKS

Heiligman, Deborah. *Celebrate Easter with Colored Eggs, Flowers, and Prayer.* Washington, DC: National Geographic Children's Books, 2007.

Tegen, Katherine. *The Story of the Easter Bunny.* New York: HarperCollins, 2005.

WEB SITES

Visit our Web site for lots of links about Easter bunnies: *childsworld.com/links*

Note to Parents, Teachers, and Librarians: We routinely verify our Web links to make sure they are safe, active sites—so encourage your readers to check them out!

Index

About the Author

Patrick Merrick was born in California and spent much of his early life moving from town to town and from state to state. Eventually, his family settled in Sioux Falls, South Dakota. In addition to writing more than 45 children's books, Patrick has been teaching science to children for more than a decade. Patrick lives in southern Minnesota with his wife and five children. When not busy with school, writing, or parenting, Patrick enjoys the occasional nap.